Libraries
ReadLearnConnect

THIS BOOK IS PART OF
ISLINGTON READS BOOKSWAP
SCHEME

Please take this book and either return it to a
Bookswap site or replace with one of your own
books that you would like to share.

If you enjoy this book, why not join your local
Islington Library and borrow more like it for free?

Find out about our FREE e-book,
e-audio, newspaper and
magazine apps, activities for
pre-school children and other
services we have to offer at
www.islington.gov.uk/libraries

ISLINGTON
For a more equal future

WORSHIP WITH ME

At the

MANDIR

By Shalini Vallepur

BookLife
PUBLISHING

©2020
BookLife Publishing Ltd.
King's Lynn
Norfolk PE30 4LS

A catalogue record for this
book is available from the
British Library.

ISBN: 978-1-78637-970-2

Written by:
Shalini Vallepur

Edited by:
Madeline Tyler

Designed by:
Dan Scase

Photo Credits

All images courtesy of Shutterstock.com.
With thanks to Getty Images, Thinkstock Photo
and iStockphoto.
Header font throughout – Shtonado. Front Cover
– L-astro, robuart, asantosg, StockSmartStart. 4&5
– NotionPic, MuchMania. 6&7 – robuart. 8&9 – jo
Crebbin, Satish Parashar, saravector, Satish Parashar.
10&11 – Sapann Design, CharacterFamily, saiko3p.
12&13 – Ken Wieland, Radiokafka, AdiiT520, Promart,
KuwarOnline, Dipak Shelare, Rudra Narayan Mitra.
14&15 – Sundeep Bhamra, CHEN WS. 16&17 – Dr
Arindam, Vectomart, Feaspb, Dr Arindam. 18&19 –
Graficshop, anand pathak, StockImageFactory.com,
13FTStudio. 20&21 – Ankit M, Jayakumar. 22&23 –
saiko3p, I Wei Huang, Ihor Pasternak, Jayakumar

CONTENTS

Words that look like <u>this</u> can be found in the glossary on page 24.

WORSHIP

With Me

Namaste! That means 'hello' in <u>Hindi</u>. I'm a pujari at a mandir and I'll be showing you around. Pujaris wear <u>tilakas</u>, like the one on my forehead, as a sign of worship.

Shiva

Have you ever been to a mandir? A mandir is a building of <u>worship</u> for followers of Hinduism, who are called Hindus. Hinduism began in India over 4,000 years ago.

Pujaris carry out <u>rituals</u> at the mandir. Hindus believe in many gods and goddesses. The <u>supreme</u> god Brahman is made up of many gods. Brahma, Shiva and Vishnu are some of these gods.

Vishnu

Brahma

Everybody is welcome in a mandir!

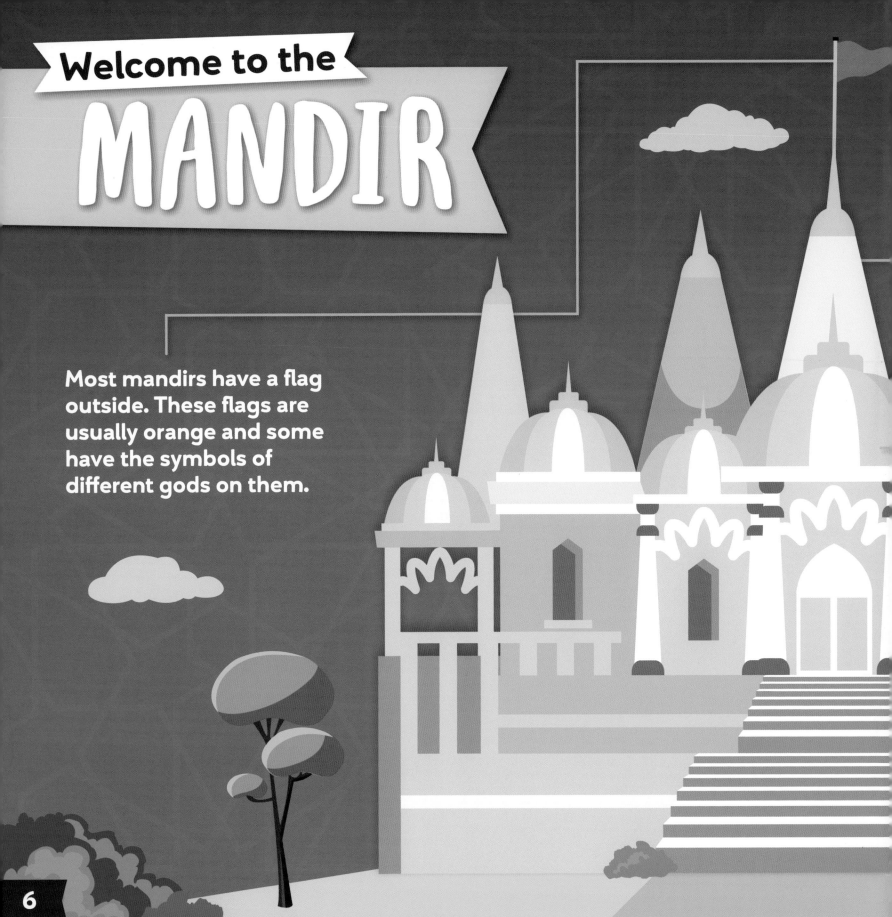

Welcome to the
MANDIR

Most mandirs have a flag outside. These flags are usually orange and some have the symbols of different gods on them.

The Front PORCH

It is important to be clean before you go inside a mandir. Some mandirs have a place outside where people can wash their feet.

Many mandirs have a big bell or bells at the entrance.
Worshippers ring the bell when they go in and out of the mandir.

INSIDE
the Mandir

People usually wear clothes that cover their arms and legs when they go to the mandir. When you enter a mandir, you must take off your shoes.

Mandirs are usually <u>dedicated</u> to a certain god or gods. In the main hall is a big <u>shrine</u> to the particular god or gods.

There are lots of smaller shrines dedicated to other gods around the main hall or in different rooms.

SHRINE AND ALTAR

There is an <u>altar</u> at most shrines.
Most altars have a bell, <u>incense</u> and lamps.

Incense

Altar

I ring the bell to let the god know that worship is starting.

Bell

A food <u>offering</u> of rice, fruit or butter is sometimes made during worship. This is called Prasada. The food is brought to the altar on a special plate, to be blessed and given to the god.

MURTIS

Shrines usually have one murti. Murtis are statues of the gods and goddesses. Worshippers try to visit all the shrines and murtis in the mandir.

The main shrine is called the garbhagriha. It may have walls around it. In some mandirs, only the pujaris are allowed near the murtis of the garbhagriha. When the worshippers reach the garbhagriha, they walk around it.

Can you see that there is space to walk around the garbhagriha?

15

PUJA

Puja is the worship that happens at the mandir. Worshippers sit in front of the garbhagriha. Incense is burnt and lamps are lit. Pujaris chant <u>mantras</u> in <u>Sanskrit</u> in front of the shrine.

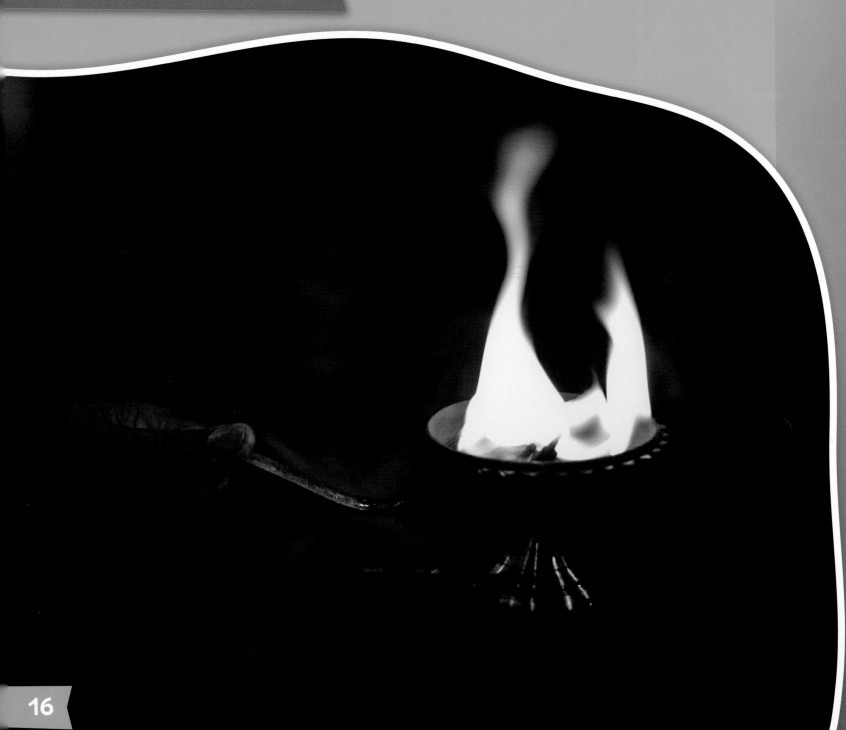

The pujari waves a lamp around the shrine, the murti and the worshippers. This is called aarti. Worshippers hold their hands in front of the flame to receive blessings.

It's important to be careful when you're near a flame, and never do this without a grown-up.

There are no set times for puja but it usually happens around sunrise, midday, sunset and midnight at the mandir.

Hindus don't have to worship at the mandir all the time, and many choose to worship at home.

Many Hindus worship at home. They may have a small shrine in their homes with their own small murtis, bells and incense.

The gods are sometimes dressed in flowers during puja.

19

NAVARATHIRI

Navarathiri is a nine-day festival that celebrates when the Goddess Durga defeated the <u>demon</u> Mahishasura.

Little statues called golu are placed in some mandirs. Many people celebrate by doing a dance called Dandiya with special sticks.

21

Many
MANDIRS

Hindus live in many different countries and there are lots of different types of mandir. Take a look at some mandirs from around the world.

Mandir in Java, Indonesia

Mandir in Chennai, South India

Mandir in Kuala Lumpur, Malaysia

Mandir in London, England

23

GLOSSARY

altar	a table or surface used to make offerings to gods or goddesses
dedicated	when something is made or done for a certain thing or person
demon	a being that goes against the gods
Hindi	a common language spoken in India
incense	something that is burnt to make a nice smell
mantras	holy words or sounds that are sung or said in prayer
offering	something that is given as a gift to gods or goddesses
rituals	actions that take place during religious ceremonies, carried out in a particular order
Sanskrit	a very old language from India
shrine	an area made for worship that is dedicated to a god or gods
supreme	the greatest
tilakas	marks that come in different shapes and colours that are made using powders or pastes and applied to the foreheads of Hindu worshippers
worship	a religious act where a person shows their love for a god or gods

INDEX

24